# Doris

# Duke's

# Shangri La

*Sharon Littlefield*

*Introduction by Carol Bier*

HONOLULU ACADEMY OF ARTS

DORIS DUKE FOUNDATION FOR ISLAMIC ART

PUBLISHED BY

Doris Duke Foundation for Islamic Art
4055 Papu Circle
Honolulu, Hawai'i 96816
Tel: 808 734-1941
www.shangrilahawaii.org

IN ASSOCIATION WITH

Honolulu Academy of Arts
900 South Beretania Street
Honolulu, Hawai'i 96814-1495
Tel: 808 532-8700
www.honoluluacademy.org

Second printing 2005
Third printing 2008

ISBN 0-937426-57-1
LCCN 2002111968

Unless otherwise indicated, photos are courtesy of
the Doris Duke Charitable Foundation Archives,
Duke Farms, Hillsborough, New Jersey. Illustrations
from the following collections are used with permis-
sion: Hawai'i State Archives; Newport Restoration
Foundation, Newport, Rhode Island; Vogue, Condé
Nast Publications Inc.; Sotheby's London.

Shuzo Uemoto, of the Honolulu Academy of Arts,
provided copystand work for illustrations on
pages 35, 41, 47, 58.

Designed and produced by Barbara Pope
Book Design

Printed in Japan

BACK COVER
*From "Ode to a Garden Carpet," by an unknown
Sufi poet, c. 1500, quoted in* Survey of Persian Art,
*vol. 14 [1967], 3184–85.*

PAGE I AND PAGE XXII
*Wall panel (detail). New Delhi and Agra, India,
1935–1938. Marble, semiprecious stone, Master
Bathroom, 41.49. David Franzen.*

PAGE II
*Doris Duke at Shangri La, c. 1939. Martin Munkácsi.*

PAGE V
*Doris Duke and Sam Kahanamoku in front of the
Playhouse at Shangri La, c. 1938–39.*

PAGE VI
*Among the technical innovations at Shangri La were
a hydraulically operated diving board and a diving
platform, c. 1938.*

PAGE VIII
*Doris Duke and Sam Kahanamoku play guitars
at Shangri La in 1939. Martin Munkácsi.*

PAGE IX
*Carpet (detail). French & Co., twentieth century.
Wool, Master Bedroom, 81.12. Shuzo Uemoto.*

PAGE X
*Doris Duke and James Cromwell pose by the Jali Pavilion
at Shangri La in 1939. Martin Munkácsi.*

PAGE XI
*Doris Duke and her crew await the start of a canoe race,
c. 1936–37. From left: Sam Kahanamoku, Doris Duke,
Bill Kahanamoku, Sarge Kahanamoku. Nate Farbman/
Hawai'i State Archives.*

# Acknowledgments

*Joan Spero*

President
Doris Duke Foundation
for Islamic Art

*Deborah Pope*

Executive Director
Shangri La

Many people have contributed to fulfilling Doris Duke's wish to open Shangri La to the public. We take pleasure in thanking James F. Gill, Chair of the Doris Duke Foundation for Islamic Art, and all the Trustees for their leadership and support, with special thanks to the late J. Carter Brown III. For their partnership in the public opening of Doris Duke's collection of Islamic art we thank George Ellis, President and Director of the Honolulu Academy of Arts, Samuel A. Cooke, Chairman of the Board, and the Academy Trustees. For their roles in early planning efforts, thanks to Barnes Riznik, Jim Stubenberg, and Foundation staff Patrick Lerch, Betsy Fader, and Alan Altschuler. Thanks also to Marianna Shreve Simpson, who oversaw curatorial and conservation efforts from 1997 to 2001; Sharon Littlefield and Anne Hayashi, who catalogued the collections; conservator Laura Gorman; and Don Hibbard, whose architectural history of Shangri La has guided much of our recent work.

During 2001 and 2002, preservation and repairs were overseen by Mason Architects, Heath Construction Services, Shangri La building and grounds manager Brian Groelsma, and their able crews. Collections manager Owen Moore oversaw extensive work on the collections and coordinated the often Herculean efforts of conservators Laura Gorman, Ann Svenson Perlman, Larry Pace, Greg Thomas, and collections technicians Simonette de la Torre, Sahra Indio, Linda Gué, and Mike Jones.

Curator Sharon Littlefield's research and writing has shaped our understanding of Shangri La, the collections of Islamic art, and Doris Duke as a collector, themes she develops in this book. In her Introduction, Islamic scholar Carol Bier brought clarity and insight to the significance of Shangri La in the life of Doris Duke. Atiqa Hachimi assisted with translating inscriptions on artwork. Photographers David Franzen and Shuzo Uemoto and book designer Barbara Pope have captured the essence of Shangri La. Thanks to Doris Duke Charitable Foundation archivists Elizabeth Steinberg and Chris Carden and to the staffs of the Bishop Museum Archives and the Hawai'i State Archives for facilitating research.

Finally, we thank Doris Duke's Hawai'i friends and former employees, who helped us enter her world and understand her passion for Islamic art and Hawai'i. Special thanks to Jinadasa de Silva, Violet Mimaki, Johnny Gomez (1908–1999), Emma Veary, Jim Nabors, and Jason Ferreira for their aloha and generosity.

# Introduction

*by Carol Bier*

$S$HANGRI LA, the most intimate of Doris Duke's residences, is the one that today offers the best view into the private domain of a public celebrity. What it reveals about Doris Duke presents a strong contrast to her well-publicized persona as a tobacco heiress, born to wealth, who liked to frolic. Observe the house, spilling down terraces of Ka'alāwai toward the sea; contemplate its well-considered vistas and its polished black lava, white marble, and coral limestone surfaces. Admire the architectural features shipped from abroad and installed on site; experience the gardens with their towering trees, sparkling water chutes, and placid walkways. It might seem that the public appearance is merely reinforced by such extravagant splendor. But look again at the collections of Islamic art glistening in the sun or peeking through mottled shade in the courtyards and columned porticos, and you may catch a glimpse of Doris Duke's passion for beauty that is pure form, whether in nature or in art.

Doris Duke had a penchant for privacy, and she found privacy in Hawai'i. Arriving for the first time in 1935 in the final stop of an around-the-world honeymoon voyage, Duke decided to stay awhile. Four months later she returned to the mainland, but fond recollections of the climate and relaxed lifestyle of Hawai'i drew her back to what would become a lifelong interest in fashioning an environment in which to enjoy quiet relaxation and private reflection amid her collection of Islamic art set within Hawai'i's gentle breezes and tropical foliage. Doris Duke was extremely reluctant, even fearful, to share aspects of her personal life. She reportedly learned early on, perhaps from her father, the stern dictum, "Trust no one." As a result, perhaps, she has been characterized as misanthropic, a view to which she undoubtedly contributed on occasion. But one aspect of her personal life emerges clearly: that Shangri La was her special place of retreat, where she could keep the world at bay.

We do not know what sparked Doris Duke's interest in Islamic art. The startling juxtaposition of Islamic tile panels, glass vessels, metalwork, and luxurious textiles with Hawai'i's luscious flora at first seems to be an anomaly. Duke herself explained it as a coincidence, a sort of falling in love twice at once—with Hawai'i and with arts of the Middle East and India. Her initial exposure to Islamic art may have come through visiting exhibitions in Europe with her father, James Buchanan Duke, who died when she was twelve years old. Together, they may have traveled to the trend-setting international expositions in London or Paris, which fed a taste for the exotic. Doris undoubtedly also accompanied her parents on visits to their neighbors, families of New York's high society whose residences held, in addition to European paintings and sculpture, the more exotic yet fashionable Moorish rooms (the Tiffany family), Islamic glass (the Moores), Hispano-Moresque ceramics (the Havemayors), Persian rooms (the Rockefellers), Moroccan ensembles, and Turkish corners. These families were also major donors to the Metropolitan Museum of Art, whose Islamic collection opened to the public in 1932 across the street from Doris Duke's family residence. The grandiose Burlington House exhibition of Persian art in London took place in 1931, when Doris was there with her mother. That exhibition was orchestrated by Arthur Upham Pope, a man known both for his charismatic personality and for his vigorous promotion of Persian arts and culture. He encouraged visitors to the immense display to partake of beauty, ignoring the particulars. Trained in philosophy with an interest in aesthetics, Pope was a forceful advocate for the understanding of Persian art as an art of pure form, articulating "tidal rhythms" that transcended cultural specificity.

What we do know is that soon after her honeymoon and before her Iranian sojourn in 1938, which was organized by Pope, Doris Duke was already predisposed to Persian architectural forms in planning the construction of her new home in Hawai'i, which was soon dubbed Shangri La. The seventeenth-century palace of the Chihil Sutun ("Forty Columns," of which twenty were reflected in the adjacent pool) in Isfahan, Iran, inspired the design for the Playhouse. A nearby palace in Isfahan is that of Ali Qapu, whose name in Persian sounds like the Hawaiian Hale Kapu (Tabu House), which reputedly is the first name Duke bestowed upon her idyll in the Pacific. Shangri La is an imaginary distant land, the hidden paradise, in James Hilton's novel, *Lost Horizon*, which was published to critical acclaim in 1933 and appeared as a film in 1937. The fantastic sets included a tiered lamasery (Tibetan monastery) descending a steep hillside with terraces, which may have captivated Duke, who was an aficionado of new movies. The public response to *Lost Horizon* was so great that "Shangri La" came to evoke a paradise on earth, or an area whose name or location is unknown or kept secret. The name "Shangri La" conjures up a mythical place of perfect living, inaccessible to others—and not inconsistent with Duke's personal inclinations.

The banyan tree and date palms, still seen today, were among the earliest plantings. Offering privacy, the high walls and shade trees may themselves express Persian conceptions of the enclosed garden, solitude, and beauty. But they also contributed to the mystique surrounding the celebrated life of Doris Duke. The ambiguity

of the blending of Hawaiian and Islamic forms is reinforced by the intimate and magical ways in which exterior and interior contrast and combine. Duke herself characterized the interior decor as a "sort of Arabian Nights." In truth, it is a rather fantastic amalgamation of artifacts drawn from India, Iran, Turkey (Istanbul), Syria (Damascus), Egypt (Cairo), Spain, and North Africa. A critic once described the residence as far smaller than the sum of its parts, claiming that it represented nothing more than ostentatious spending. Others consider the whole to be far grander than the sum of its individual components. The sequence of L-shaped rooms, interlaced with courtyards and patios, contributes to a sense of surprise and delight, enhanced by the careful placement of a set of Persian tiles here, or a Moorish hearth there. The niches lined with rich silks and velvets lend a sense of opulence and luxury within which objects of glass and metalwork glint and glisten in the sun, capturing the effects of light. The oversized leaves, the play of light and shade, and the sounds of trickling water against the backdrop of waves breaking on the shore below all contribute to the total atmosphere and stunning visual effect. In a sense, the house, the gardens, and the collection form a unified whole in which each category is inseparable from the others.

Doris Duke seems to have selected objects quickly but carefully with a vision toward the whole, the details of which changed over time, while the overall conception remained the same: to immerse herself in beauty. What she created is a confection that defies cultural specificity except in the broadest sense that it is Islamic in style, and one that addresses fundamental human concerns with forms of the imagination, evoking times long past and distant lands. She was not reluctant to drape contemporary fabrics from the bazaars of the Middle East and India in rooms resplendent with antiques and historical artifacts. She methodically retained all receipts for purchase, shipment, restoration, and installation of objects, but she did not see fit to label the works with historical or cultural data, as in a museum installation. Nor did she have any reservations about re-creating architectural features to complement those she imported (columns, fountains, floors, ceilings) and to build them into the structure of her home. It is a fabricated environment, unconstrained by the taxonomies and organizing principles of museum exhibitions and academic disciplines. The groupings of objects respect the integrity of historical cultural traditions only in the broadest general sense. There is an Orientalist quality to her efforts, which reveal the perspective of an outsider to the Islamic tradition, external to the meanings these objects may have held within the Islamic world itself, and sometimes contradictory—as in the case of the *mihrāb* (prayer niche), used to orient Muslims in prayer, installed at Shangri La for its aesthetic interest. But the blending of past and present, of Islamic cultural artifacts with

Side table (*Kursī*).

CAIRO, EGYPT, OR SYRIA, c. 1900. Copper alloy, silver, 86.0 x 47.0 cm (33⅞ x 18½ inches). Living Room, 54.136.1.

*This hexagonal stand may originally have been used to support the Qur'an as it was read. For protection, the Qur'an could be stored inside the stand by opening the small doors and placing the text within.*

Shuzo Uemoto

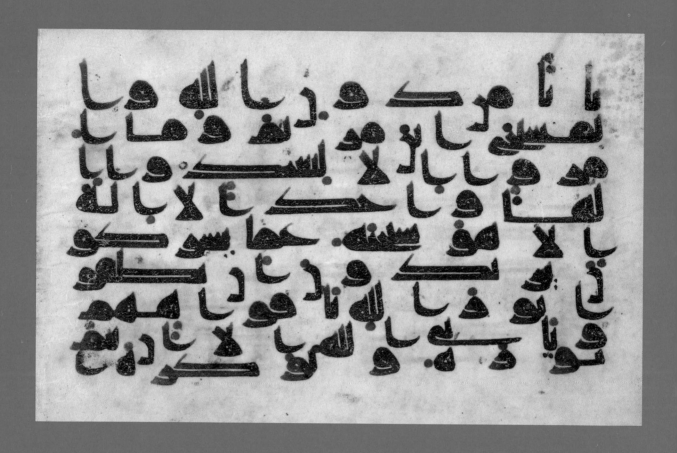

Folio from the Qur'an,
*Sura* 9, "Repentance"
(al-Tauba), verses 31–32.

NORTH AFRICA OR NEAR EAST,
c. 900. Ink and watercolor
on parchment, 10.5 x 15.6 cm
(4⅛ x 6⅛ in), Master Bedroom, 11.25.

*Calligraphy (beautiful
writing) has been a preemi-
nent Islamic art since the
seventh century, when the
Qur'an was revealed to
Muhammad and recorded
in the Arabic language.
Muslims believe that the
Qur'an is the literal Word
of God, and the written
word, because of its
association with the
copying of this sacred
text, has acquired special
significance. Controlled,
angular lettering called
Kufic script was commonly
employed in early Qur'rans.*

*Shuzo Uemoto*

Hawai'i's volcanic seascape, may also be seen as a distant expres-
sion of the early modernism that was evolving in the 1930s on the
American mainland and in Europe. One architectural historian
cites the then-current style of "Romano-Spanish-Moorish" as
"neither this nor that, but it is modern." The awe-inspiring engi-
neering feats and mechanical devices at Shangri La, such as the
retractable glass wall of the living room, the suspended doors to
the bedroom, and the diving board with its hydraulic lift, clearly
speak of Duke's fascination with new possibilities of industrial
applications, perhaps inspired by exhibits at world's fairs.

This was not her only engagement with modernism, nor was the
eclectic display of Islamic art her only engagement with the beauty
of pure form. Other of her enduring passions suggest that Doris
Duke relished being at the front line of cultural trends, even at her
far-off Hawaiian retreat: she loved playing jazz piano, she studied
many traditional forms of dance and meditation, and she expressed
dedicated horticultural interest in the breeding of orchids. The vast
collection of Islamic art at Shangri La suggests that Doris Duke
was a collector, but she may never have considered herself as
such, except in hindsight. We do know that she prided herself on
recognizing both quality and value, a trait shared with her father,
whom she adored. Although we don't know what first inspired her

to acquire Islamic art, once she began, her purchases were extensive and deliberate. The huge ceramic, luster-glazed *mihrāb* from
Veramin, Iran, was purchased in 1941 from a New York dealer. Her
earliest purchases were made in India, and later she bought from
dealers in Teheran and Damascus, introduced to her by Arthur
Upham Pope.

Throughout her adult life, Duke not only acquired large quanti-
ties of materials, but she was also intimately involved in decisions
pertaining to their installation and display. Frequently, she would
hire local craftsmen to reconstruct traditional techniques, as for
the setting of tile or the cutting of marble. Nearly every year, her
time in Hawai'i would involve relocating and reinstalling works of
art throughout the residence and engaging the design of new addi-
tions for recent purchases. The pace of her acquisitions was known
only to a privileged few, who must have staunchly honored wishes
for confidentiality, for her amassing of Islamic art over six decades
remained a very well-kept secret even when measured against the
standards of a characteristically secretive art world.

Shangri La remained the private domain of Doris Duke for
as long as she lived. She died in 1993, leaving a will in which she
stipulated the establishment of a foundation for Islamic art for
the study of Middle Eastern art and culture—a broad mandate
to share her accumulated wealth, as well as to extend the range
of understanding of the cultural meanings of these works of art.
Architectural features, such as fountains, pavilions, pools, painted
ceilings, and courtyards with columned porticos, may bring to mind
royal palaces and pavilions of the Islamic and pre-Islamic Near
East, but they also may evoke images of Paradise, vividly described
in the Qur'an, the book of recitations considered by Muslims to
be divine revelation conveyed to the Prophet Muhammad in the
seventh century of our era, as well as in Persian lyrical poetry of
later centuries. Was Doris Duke conscious of these architectural,
religious, and literary allusions? Just how culturally aware was she
in the careful selection, placement, and juxtaposition of objects
from the Near East of her own time and the far distant past? Did
she intentionally make reference to culturally specific meanings
and metaphors of Paradise to frame her life, even though these
were so far from her own reality?

Perhaps we will never know the answers to these questions, but
today's visitors to Shangri La may find apt the oft-quoted final lines
of a poem by one of Persia's great poets: "If there be a Paradise on
Earth, it is here, it is here, it is here!"

**overleaf**
*For generations of
Hawaiians, Shangri La
has been seen only from
this ocean vantage point.
Though prominently
located along a popular
public beach, the estate
is concealed by a lava
rock-veneered seawall
and by dense vegetation
that surrounds the unob-
trusive buildings nestled
in the terraced hillside.*

*David Franzen*

# Shangri La

## Islamic Art in a Honolulu Home

*Sharon Littlefield*

# Creating Shangri La —————

Doris Duke was only twenty-two years old when she envisioned Shangri La. It was 1935, the same year she married and embarked on a honeymoon tour of the world, a trip that profoundly affected the rest of her life. She traveled to eastern destinations such as Egypt, India, Indonesia, and China for the first time and became fascinated by the rich cultural traditions, in particular the Islamic ones, she encountered. In the course of the trip, Duke began to collect works of art for the Florida home she and her husband, James Cromwell, expected to occupy. But the young couple's final stop on their honeymoon, in what was then the U.S. Territory of Hawai'i, made an equally powerful impression. Indeed, the newly-weds extended their stay in Honolulu by several weeks, so pleased were they by the friends they made and the landscapes they viewed. Within months of returning from her honeymoon, inspired by her travels, Duke decided to build a home in Honolulu, where she felt comfortable and relaxed, and to fill it with Islamic art and architecture, the aesthetics of which she so keenly admired. Together, this pairing of cultures was her "Shangri La," and her estate came to be called by this name, which evokes an idyllic world.

Duke's interest in Hawaiian and Islamic cultures was far removed from the East Coast social circle in which she was raised. Born in New York City on November 22, 1912, Doris Duke was the only child of well-known entrepreneur James Buchanan Duke and Nanaline Holt Inman Duke. By the time his daughter was born, J. B. Duke had already amassed an enormous fortune, as a founder of the American Tobacco Company and Duke Energy Company. His financial success propelled the Dukes into the society of the Vanderbilts, Astors, and other wealthy families of the industrial age. Doris Duke's position was one of privilege, and her life was, consequently, of great public interest. It was said that, as her father's primary beneficiary, she would be the wealthiest heir in America. The prediction was tested sooner than anyone expected. J. B. Duke died in 1925, when his daughter was still a young girl, and she did indeed inherit the bulk of his estate.

The press dubbed Duke "the richest girl in the world" following her father's death, a sobriquet of both sympathy and censure. Yet this new identity provided Duke with a rare independence for a woman of her time. Adventurous, intelligent, and independent,

*Doris Duke at the Moti Mosque in Agra, India, c. 1935.*

3

Doris Duke.

JOHN DE COSTA, NEWPORT,
RHODE ISLAND, 1924.
Oil on canvas, 165.1 x 128.9 cm
(65 x 48 in), Newport Restoration
Foundation, 1999.653.

*Doris Duke was twelve
when she unenthusiastically
posed for this portrait at
her family home, Rough
Point, in Newport, Rhode
Island. Required to sit for
the artist each day, Duke
was unable to indulge in
her passion for swimming
in the ocean and building
sandcastles on the beach.
Her love for the ocean
and for living outdoors
contributed to her decision
to build a home in Hawai'i.*

*Newport Restoration Foundation,
Newport, Rhode Island*

Duke was determined not to be defined by social expectations or
her wealth. She enjoyed the freedom her wealth provided, pursuing
many interests including travel, the arts, historic preservation, and
environmental conservation. And she built Shangri La, a home that
would serve as her place of retreat and creative self-expression.

Duke's youthful passions for Islamic art and for Hawai'i proved
enduring. She maintained her love of living in Honolulu, and she
continued to collect Islamic art for Shangri La until her death in
1993 at the age of eighty. A philanthropist at heart, Duke provided in
her will for the creation of the Doris Duke Foundation for Islamic
Art to own Shangri La and to "promote the study and understanding
of Middle Eastern art and culture" and to "make this property available to scholars, students and others interested in the furtherance
and preservation of Islamic art and make the premises open to the
public."[1] Today, under the shadow of Diamond Head, Shangri La's
doors are open.

# Inspiration and Construction ——

Doris Duke appeared at many of the social events in which a young woman of means was expected to participate. Through them she met James Cromwell, whose mother, Eva, had married into the socially prominent Stotesbury family of Philadelphia. In 1935, after a five-year acquaintance, Duke and Cromwell were quietly married in the living room of her New York mansion. The couple boarded an ocean liner for a ten-month honeymoon tour of the world.

According to letters written by Cromwell during the couple's trip, Duke was thoroughly intrigued by her visit to India. In particular, she was excited by her visit to the Taj Mahal, the mausoleum built in the city of Agra under the patronage of the fifth Mughal emperor, Shah Jahan, c. 1631–47. James Cromwell wrote that his bride "had fallen in love with the Taj Mahal and all the beautiful marble tile, with their lovely floral designs with some precious stones."[2] Duke's reaction was so profound that she immediately commissioned a marble bedroom and bathroom suite for herself, inspired by the techniques and designs of the Taj Mahal. The suite included numerous carved marble doorways, door and window *jali*s (lattice screens), and wall and floor panels from C. G. and F. B. Blomfield, a British architectural firm based in New Delhi.

*Doris Duke and James Cromwell in Honolulu, Hawai'i, c. 1935.*

*Nate Farbman/Hawai'i State Archives*

*The Taj Mahal in Agra, India, was a major destination for Doris Duke and her husband on their honeymoon tour of the world in 1935. The legendary tomb captured her imagination so strongly that it spurred a lifelong passion for Islamic art and architecture.*

*Doris Duke*

Like the Taj Mahal itself, Duke's white marble suite was inlaid with semiprecious stones, including lapis lazuli, jade, and malachite.[3] Her appreciation of the surface detailing on the Taj characterizes her appreciation of Islamic art in general. She was less attracted to the building's romantic legends, domes, and arches than to the beauty of its inlaid ornamentation and the play of light across its marble surfaces. As architectural historian Kazi Ashraf has noted, "if Miss Duke was enamored by the Taj Mahal, it was a sensible and sophisticated gesture on her part that she did not opt for the form, in a sort of naive fantasy in Brighton or Iranistan fashion, but for the sensuality and tactility of marble, its aura in the interior, with the nuanced lighting behind the marble screens."[4] Throughout her life, Duke seems to have been drawn especially to the surface patterns, textures, and play of light characteristic of Islamic art.

The Cromwells departed India soon after placing their sizable order, but they maintained a close watch on the designs Blomfield produced in the subsequent months, and they frequently requested amendments to his proposals. While in Singapore, Cromwell wrote to Blomfield, "Mrs. Cromwell was disturbed about the panel design of the jalis shown on your rough sketch as she wanted them without panels like the jalis surrounding the [tomb] of Mumtaz at the Taj."[5]

*Inspired by her visit to the Taj Mahal, Doris Duke commissioned a bedroom and bathroom suite that echoed the surface patterns found on the seventeenth-century tomb. The suite includes arched doorways, jalis, and wall panels carved from white marble and inlaid with semi-precious stones.*

Doris Duke intended to install her marble suite in El Mirasol, the mansion owned by the Stotesbury family in Palm Beach, Florida. Her mother-in-law, Eva Stotesbury, hired architect Maurice Fatio to design the addition, and plans were already unfolding by August 1935, when the young couple arrived at their final honeymoon destination, Honolulu. They planned to stay only for a few weeks, but they extended their visit to four months. As the *Honolulu Advertiser* reported on September 19, 1935:

*Both [the Cromwells] are enthusiastic about Honolulu. "It's the most delightful place we've found in our seven months of honeymooning around the world," they declared. This is the first place they have visited where they chose to remain beyond their usual stop-over for sightseeing. . . . Honolulu has made a hit with the Cromwells— because it has left them alone.[6]*

Indeed, the quiet Hawaiian social scene proved so appealing that Duke decided to build an estate on O'ahu instead of adding on to El Mirasol. She later explained:

*The idea of building a Near Eastern house in Honolulu may seem fantastic to many. But precisely at the time I fell in love with Hawaii and I decided I could never live anywhere else, a Mogul-inspired bedroom and bathroom planned for another house was being completed for me in India so there was nothing to do but have it shipped to Hawaii and build a house around it.* [7]

Plans for the design and construction of Shangri La began almost immediately. In April 1936 Duke purchased a spectacular, 4.9-acre piece of oceanfront property at Kaʻalāwai with dramatic, sweeping views of Diamond Head and the Pacific Ocean. It was the same spot where, during their honeymoon, she and her husband, together with their new Hawaiian friends the Kahanamoku family, had spent pleasurable days picnicking, surfing, and swimming. [8] By May the architectural firm Wyeth & King had been retained to design the estate and its grounds. James Cromwell wrote in a letter that the house would "more or less copy the Hispano-Moresque style" of the Stotesbury mansion in Palm Beach. [9] Duke, architect Marion Sims Wyeth, and design supervisor Drew Baker made the long sea voyage to Hawaiʻi to create and revise renderings for the estate on site.

In February 1937 the final plans were approved, and construction began the next month. The scale of the building project received considerable attention in Hawaiʻi's newspapers. [10] According to the *Honolulu Star Bulletin*, about one hundred fifty workmen were involved in the construction of Shangri La. [11] The cost of the project,

*Shangri La was built in an area traditionally known as Kaʻalāwai. Literally translated as "the water basalt," the name refers to the porous stone that characterizes this lovely stretch of the Oʻahu coast. Doris Duke's friend Anna Furtado Kahanamoku once described Kaʻalāwai as "quite a large place on the beach. There wasn't a house there then, just a little shack. Before she built her home, she used to go out there to picnic. There was just grass and trees and she was planning to build her home there."*

*Doris Duke, James Cromwell, and David Kahanamoku fish in the ocean below Shangri La in 1939.*

Martin Munkácsi

**opposite top**
*During her honeymoon stay in Hawai'i, Doris Duke became fast friends with the multitalented and athletic Kahanamoku family. They formed the nucleus of her social circle for many years. From left: Shangri La's architect Marion Sims Wyeth, Bill, Anna, and Sam Kahanamoku, Doris Duke, David, Bernice, and Duke Kahanamoku, and an unidentified woman, c. 1937.*

$1.4 million, may seem modest by today's standards, but was impressive for Hawai'i at that time.

By 1938 Shangri La was essentially built, and Duke and her husband moved in on Christmas day. Duke, separated from her husband in 1940, used Shangri La as a seasonal home thereafter and was typically in residence during the winter months. For the rest of the year, she divided her time among other residences. Duke had inherited several homes from her father, including a mansion in New York City, Rough Point in Newport, Rhode Island, and Duke Farms in Somerville, New Jersey. Later, she acquired Falcon Lair in Beverly Hills and an apartment in New York, after donating her Fifth Avenue mansion to the Institute of Fine Arts at New York University. Of all her residences, Shangri La seems to have had a unique place in Duke's life. It was the only one she built from the ground up and filled from the inside out.

Construction of Doris Duke's estate began in March 1937 and took about two years to complete. The project was the most expensive home built in the Territory of Hawai'i at the time.

*Doris Duke with the six
Kahanamoku brothers,
c. 1937. With them, she
surfed, paddled canoes,
sailed, sang and played
Hawaiian music, and
explored the islands.
From left: Sargent, Louis,
Sam, Bill (seated), Doris,
David, and Duke.*

**opposite top**
*Doris Duke and friends
on an outing, c. 1939.
Back row, from left:
unidentified man, Marian
Paschal, unidentified
woman, Anna Furtado
Kahanamoku, Doris Duke,
and Sam Kahanamoku.
Seated, from left: Sargent
Kahanamoku, unidentified
child, David Kahanamoku,
and Johnny Gomez.*

**opposite bottom**
*Posing with giant 'ape
leaves, Sam Kahanamoku
and Doris Duke ham it up
for the camera, c. 1939.*

# Design and Innovation

**opposite**
*Doris Duke and Sam
Kahanamoku at the entry
to Shangri La, c. 1939.
A bronze medalist in the
100-meter free-style swim
at the 1924 Olympics in
Paris, Sam Kahanamoku
was also an avid surfer,
paddler, musician, and a
great wit. Doris Duke and
Sam Kahanamoku were a
familiar team in Waikīkī,
where they won tandem
surfing and paddling
competitions.*


**below**
*The simple façade of the
main residence is charac-
teristic of the structure's
unobtrusive design,
c. 1939.*

Doris Duke chose to live unconventionally by blending traditions from the East Coast, Hawai'i, and the Islamic world, and the design of Shangri La reflects this idiosyncratic blend. Shangri La has no imposing entryway, no grand façade of the type one might expect to see at the home of one of America's wealthiest individuals. The estate cannot be seen from the road at all, and only tantalizing glimpses are offered to those who surf, sail, or swim along the spectacular coastline that Shangri La overlooks. The main house is approached by descending a sloping driveway that ends at a courtyard with a large, old banyan tree. The façade here presented to the visitor is deceptively humble with its simple plaster walls and ceramic tile roof. It reveals little about the size or layout of the house. Were it not for the smiling stone camels that flank the door-way, one might not know that this approach was indeed the proper mode of entry into the house.

Stepping from outside to inside, guests are presented with star-tling juxtapositions: from a plain façade to a highly ornate interior, from a tropical Hawaiian landscape to refined Islamic elegance. The effect is heightened by the diversity of Islamic artistic tradi-tions displayed in the foyer. Guests are surrounded by an array of colors produced by six hundred Iznik tiles from Turkey, eighty-four colored-glass, Spanish-style windows complemented by hints of sunlight and lamps, and opulent textiles, urns, and wood chests

*In contrast to the simple
exterior, the foyer's interior
is awash with color, light,
pattern, and texture—
an effect created through
Duke's decision to juxtapose
a great variety of Islamic
architectural and artistic
forms in the room.*

*Textiles with floral motifs
from Central Asia and
India are displayed behind
mother-of-pearl inlaid
wood chests from Syria.
Above them is a painted
wood ceiling made in
Morocco. Ceramic tiles
from Turkey cover the walls,
which are pierced with
Spanish-style colored-glass
windows. The combination
of such diverse cultural traditions within a single room
is typical of Shangri La.*

*David Franzen*

from India, Central Asia, Iran, and Syria. The understated façades
of Shangri La, in comparison to its dynamic interiors, suggest that
Duke's intent in building was not to impress her neighbors but to
please herself. Her decision to combine a great variety of objects,
brought to Hawai'i from North Africa, Central and South Asia, and
the Near and Middle East, was ingenious and bold. In retrospect,
Duke's blending of diverse Islamic traditions is just as provocative
as her juxtaposition of Hawaiian and Islamic elements at the estate.
Perhaps a reporter for the *Honolulu Star Bulletin* put it most tellingly
when he wrote in 1938, "On all the face of the globe there is no
other place like it nor is there likely to be."[12]

Leaving the foyer and walking through the house may prove
perplexing to guests at first, for doors to rooms and wings, hidden
gardens, and stairs confront the visitor at various turns. By design,
the overall layout of the estate is not symmetrical, and it does
not have a strong entry axis—either of which would help orient
guests as they explore the property. A plan reveals that Shangri La
is essentially composed of two large buildings: the low, rambling
main house and a pool/guesthouse known as the Playhouse. These
whitewashed buildings are separated by a 75-foot swimming pool

with a diving board and diving platform. The buildings and the pool run parallel to a high sea wall with a lava rock veneer, which protects the estate from the surf just beyond. A sinuous jetty was built into the ocean to shelter a yacht. On a secluded section of the property, separated from the residential areas by a tennis court, stand a modest caretaker's cottage and garage. The rest of the property is appealingly landscaped with gardens, fishponds, grass, palm trees, and other lush vegetation.

The design reflects Duke's love of swimming, surfing, sailing, and outdoor living in general. Instead of a movie theater, bowling alley, or large reading room, Shangri La features outdoor sporting opportunities: the large pool, direct access to the ocean, and tennis courts, for example. In 1939 *Life* magazine described Shangri La as "a stately concrete structure of Morocco-Persian architecture [which] stretches white and gleaming along the ocean rocks. It has only five rooms, but a swimming pool, playhouse, yacht basin and tennis court make it an ideal playground. In it, some four or five months a year, the Cromwells find a haven of quiet retreat. . . . And here, within earshot of the surf, the quiet, level-headed girl who is one of the richest heiresses in the world, fishes, swims, reads, prefers simple healthy living to social splendor."[13]

Though idiosyncratic, the plan of Shangri La does follow three main principles, all of which show sensitivity to the beauty of the surrounding Hawaiian landscape. First, the house is essentially a single story, a design which ensures that the built environment does not overwhelm the natural environment. Like the grounds,

*Shangri La is designed around a central courtyard fronted by public spaces, such as the living room, Turkish Rooms, and pool. Private spaces, such as Duke's bedroom and the staff rooms, were built along hallways connecting to the main courtyard.*

*David Franzen*

**right**

*Mihrāb* from the tomb
of Imamzada Yahya at
Veramin, Iran.

'ALI IBN MUHAMMAD IBN ABI
TAHIR, KASHAN, IRAN, DATED
SHA'BAN 663/MAY 1265.
Stone-paste, underglaze-painted
dark blue and turquoise, over-
glaze-painted luster, 384.5 x 228.6
x 21.6 cm (151⅛ x 90 x 8½ inches),
Mihrab Room, 48.327.

*A* mihrāb *is a recess
or niche in a wall that
indicates the direction of
Mecca, and therefore the
direction of prayer.
At Shangri La, Doris
Duke chose to locate the
mihrāb on an east wall,
rather than in a north-
western orientation,
which would be the
proper direction from
Hawai'i to Mecca.*

*Although this placement
indicates that Duke did not
use the mihrāb for religious
purposes, her decision to
install it in one of the most
prominent locations at
Shangri La underscores
her awareness of its widely
acknowledged aesthetic
and historical value.*

*Shuzo Uemoto*

**opposite**

*In the living room,
several of Shangri La's
most significant works
of art are visible including
the mihrāb. Other notable
ceramics include plates,
basins, and tiles made in
fifteenth- and sixteenth-
century Spain.*

*Duke purchased them
at Gimbel's in New York
City during the department
store's sale of William
Randolph Hearst's treas-
ures in the early 1940s.*

*David Franzen*

*The living room at night. Duke had special lighting installed throughout Shangri La to ensure that her collection could be viewed to best advantage day or night.*

David Franzen

*The view of the Playhouse, Diamond Head, and the Pacific Ocean is unforgettable.*

David Franzen

Among architect Marion Sims Wyeth's early proposals for the design of Shangri La was this 1936 rendering of a massive, monumental structure that turned its back on the ocean. In consultation with Duke, Wyeth eventually created a home that was far less imposing in both its form and surface ornamentation.

the main house is terraced across the property to provide variation in its appearance. Second, the rooms and wings of the main house radiate around an interior, central courtyard. This courtyard-and-wing plan provides most rooms in the house with ocean views. Third, the main structures follow the orientation of the coastline, resulting in a strong axis that visually connects key areas of the property to the Hawaiian locale by the view just beyond. Diamond Head, the Playhouse, the pool, the living room, and a magnificent luster *mihrāb* (prayer niche) that is considered Shangri La's most important work of art are all aligned on this axis. The glass wall on the west side of the living room, also on the axis, descends into the basement. When the glass wall is down, the axis is reinforced, for one can then walk through the living room onto a grassy terrace, stroll past the enormous pool, and arrive at the Playhouse, all the time admiring the sweeping ocean and mountain views beyond. A writer for the *Honolulu Star Bulletin* described Shangri La in 1938:

*There is nothing massive about the place: nothing that impresses by mere size. It is more like a perfectly cut gem with a flawless attention to detail, with a certain restraint in design that sparkles nonetheless. Its low, rambling architecture nestles against the hill behind it; its white walls sharpen the blue and green of the ocean, landscape and sky; its great brown stone retaining wall is in restful harmony with the sea that curls below it.*[14]

In addition to being a home of beauty, Shangri La was also a home of technical marvels, of which the descending glass wall in the living room is perhaps the most remarkable. It is operated electrically by an Otis Elevator system. Both conceptually and technologically, a descending wall composed of an enormous glass pane was innovative at the time it was installed at Shangri La.[15] The use of glass ensures that the beauty of the surrounding landscape, as well as the Playhouse and pool, are visible regardless of the wall's position. When the wall disappears, a dynamic blending of interior and exterior spaces occurs that is typical of much of Shangri La's design.

Another innovation Duke implemented at Shangri La was the use of sliding *jali*s. These lattice-carved screens with floral and geometric motifs were part of the marble bedroom set that Duke commissioned in India. Though based on the *jali*s seen in Mughal

**opposite**
*The Playhouse at Shangri La was modeled on the Chihil Sutun, a royal pavilion built in 1647 in Isfahan, Iran. Doris Duke most likely took this photo of her friend and adviser, Mary Crane, in front of the Chihil Sutun in 1938 when they visited the site. Duke may have felt drawn to the building's design because it blends interior and exterior spaces. The fusion of interiors and exteriors is characteristic of Shangri La.*

23

*The* jalis *in Doris Duke's bedroom slide open or shut to provide varying degrees of light, air, and privacy. In this photograph, c. 1938–39, the* jali *in the center is fully extended, while those on either side have been pushed into the pocket doorways.*

**opposite**
*The hallway to Doris Duke's bedroom includes a* lānai *(porch) and a garden with a small waterfall and koi pond. The arcade features carved marble columns, which Duke purchased in 1941 at the Hearst sales. The arcade evokes the Alhambra and other buildings erected in regions of southern Spain and northern Africa. This photograph was likely taken just after the arcade was installed in the early 1940s.*

architecture in South Asia, those at Shangri La are unique because they are not fixed in place. Instead, they and the glass doors behind them slide open or shut to provide varying degrees of light, ocean breezes, and privacy. Duke explained:

*I tried to keep the house in character, using original Near Eastern pieces, but in order to make it livable as well, it was often necessary to adapt them to uses for which they were not originally intended. Thus in my Indian bedroom, carved, cutout marble* jalis *or screens, which were formerly used by Indian princes to keep their wives from other eyes, have a new purpose: they are not only decorative, but a means of security, for they can be locked without shutting off the air, and when not wanted can be pushed back into the wall.*[16]

Various principles of Islamic domestic architecture may be seen in the plan and appearance of Shangri La, such as the unassuming façade, central courtyard, and abundance of gardens. Though Duke and her husband originally called for a "Hispano-Moresque"–style home, Shangri La's design resonates with Islamic domestic architecture from a larger sphere, especially the Middle East and North Africa. In crowded urban centers such as Cairo, for example, family homes, possessions, and lifestyles were shielded from street life by presenting a simple façade to the public. Inside, however, rooms were as elaborate as a family could afford. These urban homes were often built around inner courtyards that permitted sunlight, air, and vegetation inside. The courtyard plan was practical, for it separated female spaces from male ones and the family's private spaces from those of guests.[17]

At Shangri La also, the courtyard separates guest areas from private quarters. Wings, such as those leading to Duke's bedroom and the staff quarters, extend off the central courtyard, but are fitted with lockable doors to limit access. In contrast, rooms intended for guests' use, such as the Turkish Rooms, living room, and dining room, are connected directly to the central courtyard. The idea of separating guest areas from the owner's private spaces resonated with Duke. Her husband wrote:

*Doris is planning to construct a very large pool where the present pool is situated, and is also planning to have a sort of combination guest-house and boat-house Cabana arrangement, built on or just above the swim pool. This guest-house would probably have double guest-rooms with a [lanai] for each, a miniature kitchen and sports-room connected to the pool. We got this idea from India and the purpose, of course, is not to have our guests continually in our hair, and vice versa!*[18]

The buildings at Shangri La surround, and are surrounded by, gardens and other landscaping, another feature characteristic of Islamic architecture.[19] The Moon Garden is located at one corner of the estate. Along the length of an upper terrace is another garden, Duke's interpretation of a Mughal garden. In between the two lie the lush central courtyard, gardens near the pool and Playhouse, and a private garden adjacent to Duke's bedroom. Each area features a unique combination of still or moving water, vegetation, trees, grass, and fishponds.

To walk from one room to another, one usually traverses both interior spaces and covered exterior spaces. The numerous gardens play an important role in enhancing the exterior parts of the journey, as do particular works of art that Duke displayed outdoors. The close relationship between internal and external spaces at Shangri La is characteristic of upper-class Islamic domestic architecture and is well suited to the tropical climate of Hawai'i.

Although the main house demonstrates principles of design found within Islamic cultures, the façade of the Playhouse provides the most direct reference to a specific example of Islamic architecture. It was adapted from the Chihil Sutun, a seventeenth-century pavilion built in Isfahan, Iran, under the patronage of the Safavid emperor Shah 'Abbas II. Duke herself traveled to Isfahan in 1938 and took photographs of the Chihil Sutun to assist Marion Sims Wyeth with the design details. Mary Crane, a graduate student of Islamic art history at New York University's Institute of Fine Arts, provided extracts from seventeenth-century travelogues that described the appearance of the Chihil Sutun. Crane also reviewed manuscript illustrations from the era in search of inspiration. Over a period of six months, the two women exchanged letters reporting on their findings.[20]

opposite
*This long hallway separates Doris Duke's bedroom from the central courtyard, providing greater privacy. Note the* jali *at the end of the hall, which serves as the entry to the bedroom. The separation of public and private spaces at Shangri La is typical of Islamic domestic architecture.*

*David Franzen*

27

# Transformations ⟷

Doris Duke's estate was never truly finished. When her longtime friend Johnny Gomez was asked what year Shangri La had been finished, he laughingly replied, "Never was finished, never. There was no such word as finished."[21] Shangri La continued to evolve over the years as Duke energetically and creatively designed and redesigned her Hawaiian home whenever she acquired works of art. Sometimes her designs led to large-scale renovations that required relocating monumental works of art, such as a ceramic tile panel measuring 7 feet by 26 feet, which was once displayed outdoors but was eventually moved inside. No physical challenge was too daunting; the end product had to suit her sense of aesthetics.

In the 1960s, when Duke was in her fifties, she transformed her dining room, which was originally Hawaiian in inspiration. She described the room's original decor:

*I used marine life as the decorative motif: tanks for the brilliant fish that abound in these waters are built into one wall, and a shell collection is displayed in a second. The other two sides overlook the ocean.*[22]

The appearance of the remodeled dining room was completely different; the room now drew upon Islamic forms, like the rest of Shangri La. The large windows with their sweeping views of the ocean and Diamond Head were retained, but the tanks and shell collection were removed. They were replaced with a large, twentieth-century mosaic tile panel and an Ottoman-style fireplace. Duke furnished the renovated dining room with Egyptian and Indian cloth panels, and also selected a fabric covering for the ceiling and walls, giving the room the impression of an elaborate tent. The room evokes those Islamic cultures that favor a nomadic lifestyle and prefer portable architectural structures, such as cloth tents, to permanent buildings composed of stone or brick.

In the early 1980s, as Duke turned seventy, she oversaw another major renovation at Shangri La. She had recently acquired a mid-nineteenth-century room interior from Syria, composed of carved and painted wood panels, doors, and niches; carved and inlaid stone blocks; and other large architectural fragments. The interior had once belonged to the Quwwatlis, an aristocratic family that had resided in Damascus for seven centuries. In the 1920s, the Quwwatli family had sold the interior to the firm of Asfar & Sarkis, which

later resold it to another dealer, Hagop Kevorkian. Both were dealers whom Duke often patronized. The Kevorkian Foundation later gave this and another interior as gifts to the Metropolitan Museum of Art and to the Kevorkian Center for Near Eastern Studies at New York University.[23] Duke's room was part of the Kevorkian Center interior, and became known at Shangri La as the Turkish and Baby Turkish Rooms.

What had previously been a billiards room, a bathroom, an office on the floor above, and a ceiling in between was demolished to make room for the large interior. Duke determined that the new room ought to be sunken slightly from the adjacent central courtyard, so the existing foundation was excavated to permit a step down into the room. Dirt was piled up along the east wall as the foundation for a large marble platform that would be used as the main seating area.

Once the structural renovations were completed, marble flooring and a fountain were set down. Though both contain historic marble panels, they consist mainly of panels designed and cut by Duke and the Shangri La house staff. The last elements installed were the wooden wall panels and ceilings, whose lavender wood frames were not originally part of the Quwwatli interior, but were purchased separately. The frames were retouched and regilded as needed, and Duke herself took an active part in some of this restoration work. Estate employee Jin de Silva remembers how Duke and her artisans would sit around a table in the courtyard, working in an assembly-line manner and consulting one another about their respective tasks.[24] When the interiors were in place, ceramics, glass, metalwork, and other objects were brought from around Shangri La to the Turkish Rooms for display in the niches. Like other areas of the estate, these rooms continued to evolve. Duke enjoyed viewing, critiquing, and rearranging the portable objects in them whenever she was in Hawai'i.

In the initial stages of Shangri La's conception and construction, both Duke and Cromwell were involved in planning the estate. In the succeeding years Cromwell's influence decreased as the couple experienced marital problems; they separated in 1940 and were divorced in 1943. Architect Marion Sims Wyeth, design supervisor Drew Baker, and others also provided Duke with input. Baker was the on-site supervising architect, who remained in residence in Hawai'i for the duration of the construction. Duke, however, always relied on her own needs and tastes when reviewing designs submitted by professionals. She frequently requested amendments to ensure that the estate evolved to coincide with her vision. In her own words, "it isn't the product of any one person, but a number of architects and decorators from all over the world, finally put together by me."[25] In 1937 Robert Oliver Thompson, who jointly served as the landscape designer of Shangri La with his wife Catherine Jones Richard Thompson, met Doris Duke. When asked to describe Duke's involvement in the creation of Shangri La, he replied that she "was constantly on the job and took great interest in every tree, every leaf, twig, shrub. She certainly did. I have never seen a girl take the interest that she did and she knew what she wanted."[26]

Perhaps the most successful aspect of Shangri La's design is its understated architectural plan. Together, Wyeth and Duke decided that there should be few structural and decorative embellishments. This approach allows Shangri La's two "stars," the surrounding landscape and Duke's Islamic art collection, to shine. Indeed, it is the Islamic works of art embedded within the estate—and the way Duke chose to display them—that truly define Shangri La's unique character.

*Detail of the decorative niche (maṣab) from the Quwwatli interior, now part of the Baby Turkish Room. A prominent feature of historic Syrian interiors was an elaborate wall niche where cherished objects could be displayed. The niches were often highly ornate themselves, an effect created by juxtaposing different media such as wood, marble, and ceramic.*

**left and above**

*Details of the carved
and painted wood panels
originally in the Quwwatli
house, now in the Baby
Turkish Room.*

Shuzo Uemoto

*The Quwwatli home in
Damascus, c. 1920, pieces
of which became part
of the Turkish and Baby
Turkish Rooms at Shangri
La. The Quwwatlis were
among the richest mer-
chants in Damascus and
owned at least four homes
within the walls of the
old city.*

▼

**above and right**

*Because the preexisting spaces could not accommodate all of the wood and ceiling paneling that were part of the Quwwatli interior, Doris Duke decided to outfit two adjacent rooms at Shangri La rather than rebuild the existing structure. She named these rooms the Turkish and Baby Turkish Rooms. Though the interiors are actually Syrian in origin, Duke was probably referring to the Ottoman dynasty's rule of Damascus from their capital in Istanbul, Turkey.*

David Franzen

# Collecting Islamic Art

*Designer René Martin submitted photographs of the work Duke commissioned as it progressed in his workshop in Rabat, Morocco. Here a young boy eyes the photographer as two older men work on the living room ceiling for Shangri La, c. 1938.*

Over a period of about sixty years, Doris Duke purchased approximately thirty-five hundred objects for Shangri La. The majority can be classified as Islamic works of art. The size of her collection is considerably larger than most Islamic art collections at museums in the United States.[27] And, unlike a museum, nearly all of the collection at Shangri La is on display. Also, Duke decided to install works of art with particular architectural functions, such as ceramic door spandrels, door frames, and fireplace surrounds, in the structure of Shangri La, providing a befitting context within which to understand the original functions of the objects.

Taken as a whole, the collection underscores the diversity of Islamic cultures. For example, it includes objects produced from the early period of Islamic expansion in the seventh century, to works produced in the twentieth century. Regions such as South and Central Asia, Europe, the Near and Middle East, and North Africa are represented by the works of art, as are different lifestyles including court, city, and village. Further, a great variety of media—a celebrated aspect of Islamic art—is juxtaposed in nearly every room: wood, paper, precious and semiprecious stone, glass, ceramic, metal, and fiber.

Duke favored particular types of Islamic art, especially ceramics, which abound in both interior and exterior spaces at Shangri La. Ceramic vessels and tile panels constitute about one-fifth of the Shangri La collection. *Mina'i*-type bowls made in medieval Iran, fifteenth-century lusterware vessels from Spain, and Iznik plates produced in sixteenth-century Turkey are among the highlights of the ceramic collection. Large Iranian storage jars made as early as the eighth century are located in the central courtyard, adjacent to numerous Iranian tile panels including one hundred molded tiles from the thirteenth century and over two hundred underglaze-painted tiles from the seventeenth century.

The single most important work of art Duke purchased for Shangri La is also ceramic: the monumental *mihrāb*, or prayer niche, made in Kashan, Iran, for the tomb of Imamzada Yahya at Veramin, Iran. This *mihrāb* is significant not only for its size, but also because it is signed by the well-known potter ʿAli ibn Muhammad ibn Abi Tahir, and dated 663 A.H. (1265 A.D.) in the inscription near the bottom. After long and persistent negotiations, Duke purchased the

**Dish.**

IZNIK, TURKEY, C. 1580–85.
Stone-paste, underglaze-painted.
5.4 x 26.7cm (2⅛ x 10½ in.).
Turkish Room, 48.34.

*Chinese blue-and-white ceramics were enthusiastically collected at the Ottoman court. Local potters, particularly in the town of Iznik, soon began to produce comparable vessels. They experimented with design, shape, color, and materials, and ultimately produced a unique ceramic tradition that itself came to be imitated by others.*

*Shuzo Uemoto*

**Bowl.**

IRAN, LATE TWELFTH OR EARLY THIRTEENTH CENTURY.
Stone-paste, overglaze-painted luster and polychrome, gilding.
8.3 x 18.7 cm (3¼ x 7⅜ inches).
Mihrab Room, 48.328.

*An unusual work of art, this bowl features two different potter's techniques: luster and* mina'i. *Lusterware, named for the metallic sheen of its surface, is seen in the calligraphic band around the sides, while at center* mina'i *(a name derived from the Persian word for "enamel") is used for the figure on horseback. Both techniques were popular in medieval Iran, but were rarely combined on the same object because of the complexity of the technical processes.*

*Shuzo Uemoto*

work from Hagop Kevorkian in 1940.[28] The *mihrāb* was installed not long before the bombing of Pearl Harbor—after which it was quickly uninstalled and stored in the basement for safety. It was reinstalled after World War II. The *mihrāb* stands in one of Shangri La's most prominent locations, at the start of the central axis that extends through the living room, across the pool, down to the Playhouse, and up to Diamond Head. As Duke herself explained, "The high spot, the focal point of the house, . . . is the thirteenth-century luster tile mihrab, which is as important historically as it is artistically."[29]

In addition to ceramics, Duke's collection is strong in objects dating from the seventeenth through nineteenth centuries. Pre-dominant are courtly, aristocratic, and religious works of art made during the reigns of wealthy and influential Muslim dynasties, such as the Ottomans, Mughals, Safavids, and Qajars. No room at Shangri La is dedicated solely to the arts of a particular era, but some favor particular dynasties: Duke's bedroom recalls Mughal India, the Playhouse is replete with arts of Qajar Iran, and the central courtyard suggests Safavid Iran. The Turkish, Baby Turkish, and Damascus Rooms are largely composed of eighteenth- and nineteenth-century architectural interiors originally made for homes in Ottoman Syria.

Overall, Duke did not employ a chronological or regional display scheme when situating objects in rooms, or even in deciding which objects should be displayed in a given room. Instead, she combined and recombined the works of art into a kind of assemblage of Islamic cultures—a mixture that suited her aesthetic sense. The resulting display juxtaposes colors, media, and scale, allowing each

**page 37**
Mosaic panel.

IRAN OR CENTRAL ASIA, FIFTEENTH CENTURY.
Carved wood, 172.7 x 111.8 cm (68 x 44 in), Turkish Room, 64.16.

*Islamic art is renowned for its use of geometric decoration. Artists show a highly sophisticated under-standing of geometric prin-ciples, combining repetition, symmetry, radiating and regenerating forms, inter-lacing and overlapping forms, and negative and positive spaces to create boldly appealing patterns, as seen in this wood panel.*

*David Franzen*

**opposite and left**
*Mihrāb* from the tomb of Imamzada Yahya (details).

Mihrab Room, 48.327

*Detail at left shows the artist's signature and the date.*

*Shuzo Uemoto*

Side table (*Kursī*) (detail).

CAIRO, EGYPT, OR SYRIA,
c. 1900. Copper alloy, silver,
Living Room, 54.136.1.

*Shuzo Uemoto*

object to be seen for its individual merits at the same time that it contributes to the overall mood of a room.

In 1938, during Shangri La's construction, Doris Duke traveled to Iran, Iraq, Syria, Turkey, and Egypt to acquire works of art for her estate. Her tour was arranged by Arthur Upham Pope, one of the most distinguished scholars of Persian art of the time. Pope was intrigued by Duke's plan to build an Islamic-style house, and he wrote letters suggesting approaches to its design. His influence was limited, though, for construction was well under way by the time he became aware of the project. Still, he performed an invaluable service by facilitating Duke's 1938 travels and introducing her to several dealers, including A. Rabenou of Tehran and Paris, and Asfar & Sarkis of Damascus. Rabenou sold Duke numerous ceramic tile panels during her visit to Iran, among which was a figurative fireplace surround depicting scenes of nineteenth-century Qajar court life. Duke purchased most of the seventeenth-century tiles in the central courtyard from Rabenou, who had acquired them from a private home in Julfa, a suburb of Isfahan.[30] From Asfar & Sarkis, she purchased inlaid furniture, and later the historic interior installed in her Damascus Room. Into her mid-seventies, Duke continued to travel in the Islamic world, visiting such destinations as Pakistan, Uzbekistan, Morocco, India, Egypt, and Indonesia.

In addition to purchasing objects abroad, Duke also bought from dealers, galleries, and auction houses, mostly in New York City. For example, she purchased numerous monochrome ceramic vessels and luster star tiles from H. Khan Monif. At the Hearst sales in the 1940s, she bought Spanish and Syrian furniture, ceramics, and carved stone capitals, among other items. Eight Zand and Qajar oil paintings and a large Qajar ceiling came from various New York sales. Adolpho Loewi of Venice provided her with over six hundred Iznik tiles. Duke bought an ornate chandelier made by Baccarat in France for the Indian market from Nesle, Inc., which had purchased it from the former owner, Salar Jung of Hyderabad, India. A substantial portion of the collection was purchased at Parke-Bernet Galleries in New York City.

Although Duke had the resources to collect whatever was available, her vision of Shangri La was not limited to whatever happened to be for sale. Indeed, her approach to creating Shangri La was remarkably active and carefully considered. What she could not buy ready-made, she ordered custom-made. For example, in the initial stages of Shangri La's construction, Duke commissioned numerous, large-scale architectural installations from three sources: René Martin of Rabat, Morocco; Rabenou, who also sold her historic works of art; and the Blomfield architecture firm in New Delhi, which oversaw production of the master bedroom and bathroom suite.

Duke met René Martin through a mutual acquaintance in November 1937 while visiting Antibes, France. She made inquiries

An original receipt documents Duke's purchase of three bureaus from the dealers Asfar & Sarkis in Damascus. At the bottom of the receipt, Sarkis wrote, "7850 Syrian Piasters at the rate of 180 Syr. piast. per dollar (exchange rate of 11th August 1939)," adding, "Only: Forty three Dollars & 60/100."

Doris Duke shops for bureaus in Damascus, 1938.

ASFAR & SARKIS
DAMASCUS
SYRIA 13th October 1939

RUGS
ANTIQUITIES
OBJETS D'ART
SILKS

P. O. B. 87
PHONE 4-11

Mr. James R. H. Cromwell, New York City
630 Fifth Avenue,

| | | Syrian Piasters | |
|---|---|---|---|
| 1 | Bureau inlaid with mother of pearls | 2000 | |
| | repairs | 550 | 2550 |
| 1 | Dismantled bureau inlaid with mother of pearls | 1300 | |
| | repairs | 550 | 1850 |
| 1 | Dismantled bureau inlaid with mother of pearls | 1800 | |
| | repairs | 200 | 2000 |
| | Case | | 1450 |
| | | | 7850 |

7850 Syrian Piasters at the rate of 180 Syr. piast. per dollar (exchange rate of 11th August 1939) — $43 60/100

Only: Fourty three Dollars & 60/180

confirming the quality of the work produced in his studio and soon placed a substantial order. Shangri La's ceramic roof tile, the enormous ceiling and doors in the living room, the ceiling in the foyer, plaster archways in the living room and foyer, Cromwell's bedroom suite, and several large wood screens in the central courtyard, living room, and the Damascus and Moroccan Rooms were all commissioned from Martin. His designs appear to be based on motifs, techniques, and aesthetics popular in Moroccan palaces during the nineteenth century.[31] Martin provided preliminary sketches of his work to Wyeth, so the elements could be incorporated into the overall design of Shangri La. As she had been with Blomfield, Duke was an active patron. She met with Martin in Paris in February 1938 to request changes, and he also sent photographs to her recording the work in progress.

In a telegram to Rabenou, Pope wrote,

*Mrs. James Cromwell arriving Paris probably twenty seventh calling on you shortly thereafter very wealthy important client building house Persian style much interested mihrab both spandrels total business should be large.*[32]

*René Martin painted this watercolor to show his vision of the living room and the architectural features he would create. Doris Duke largely followed Martin's design, as shown in the early photograph opposite. However, as with all work she commissioned, Duke modified aspects to suit her own aesthetic sense. For example, she eliminated Martin's proposed woodwork above the fireplace, and moved the large wood doors from beside the sofa to the doorway that frames the* mihrāb.

*Woman Playing a Stringed Instrument.*

IRAN, C. 1800. Oil on canvas, 172.1 x 83.8 cm (67⅞ x 33 in). Playhouse, 34.6.

*Although Islamic art is often thought to be devoid of figural representation, many works of art made in the Islamic world do feature figures. Their use tends to be restricted to secular arts, such as this painting depicting Qajar court life. In contrast, religious arts—prayer rugs, mosque ornamentation, and the Qur'an—feature geometry, nature, and calligraphy.*

*Shuzo Uemoto*

In addition to purchasing historic tile panels from Rabenou, Duke also commissioned newly made ones. An enormous tile panel in the central courtyard was made in 1930s Iran, but based on two seventeenth-century tiles that flank the portal of the Shah Mosque in Isfahan.[33] Duke also commissioned large tile panels for the exteriors of the living room and Playhouse. Several photographs were taken in Iran during the production of the Shangri La tile panels, and a traveler affiliated with the American Institute for Iranian Architecture filmed the activity.[34] In February 1940, in spite of the troubles of World War II, 138 cases of tiles arrived in Hawai'i and were soon installed around Shangri La.

The process of shipping such fragile goods to Honolulu from the far corners of the earth was complicated. Obtaining permits, passing customs, and contracting sea passage required many hands and resulted in many delays. Rabenou's tiles are a good case in point. They were completed in June 1939, and it took five men more than thirty days to pack them. The boxes of tiles were driven by truck to the port city of Bushire on the Persian Gulf, a trip that typically took three days but was extended to ten to avoid damaging the cargo. By the time the tiles arrived in Bushire and the shipping permits were secured, the plan to ship them to Marseilles was abandoned. War had broken out, and commercial transport was no longer viable across the Mediterranean Sea. Faced with the

*The Playhouse consists of three rooms: two guest suites and a large living room. The living room, seen here, features important works of art made in nineteenth-century Iran during the reign of the Qajar dynasty. The oil paintings, the tile fireplace surround, and the chandelier depict scenes of court life. The ceiling, though suggestive of the same period, was fabricated in Hawai'i.*

*David Franzen*

Tile panel in the form
of a fireplace surround
(detail).

IRAN, NINETEENTH CENTURY.
Stone-paste, underglaze-painted,
Playhouse, 48.429.

*David Franzen*

possibility of storing the tiles indefinitely, Duke sought alternative forms of transport. Eventually the tiles were shipped from Iran to India, where they sat for a month in Bombay until space could be found on a ship sailing to Honolulu — by way of New York.[35]

Among the twentieth-century architectural works Duke commissioned for the estate, some were made abroad in India, Iran, and Morocco. Others, however, were custom-made in Hawai'i to resemble Islamic forms. The fiberglass ceiling in the living room of the Playhouse was painted in Hawai'i, but in an Islamic style convincing enough to prompt a well-known auction house to misidentify it as "19th century Persian" in an appraisal. The Shangri La house staff, none of whom had formal artistic training, helped make most of the Islamic-style marble floor tiles in the Turkish Rooms and the private hallway to Duke's bedroom.

The Playhouse is not the only example of a large Islamic architectural form at Shangri La that was built in Hawai'i. Across an upper terrace of her estate, Duke envisioned re-creating a Mughal garden. Taking her cue from Shalimar Garden in Lahore, Pakistan, she designed her garden as a long, narrow pathway with a water channel running down the center, plantings on either side, and *chinikhāna*s (niches for oil lamps) at one end. At night, with electric candles lit in the *chinikhāna*s, a magical effect was produced when water cascaded in front of lights and into the channel below. A series of lotus-shaped fountains runs the course of the water channel, providing additional water flow. Duke's Mughal garden mimics the four-part garden scheme typically employed in Mughal gardens in South Asia, but on a much smaller scale.

Unconventional, eclectic, idiosyncratic: these words could all be applied to Doris Duke as a collector, for she not only acquired historic works of Islamic art, but was also a patron of Islamic art, and even a creator of Islamic-style art. It is difficult to place her patterns of art collecting within a broader framework, for they correspond neither to her East Coast social circle nor to other twentieth-century collectors of Islamic art. Many successful industrialists of the age, such as J. P. Morgan, Andrew Carnegie, and A. W. Mellon, and their heirs collected art. Most purchased European art, including Old Master paintings, to fulfill time-honored notions of culture and gentility.[36] Many donated their private collections to prestigious public museums, a gesture that was both philanthropic and self-interested. Duke's decision to collect the relatively unknown art of the Islamic world and to display it in her remote Hawaiian home, where few would observe it during her lifetime, suggests a very different relationship to art.

From the perspective of many Islamic art collectors, much of Duke's collection lies outside the canon of what is typically considered a masterpiece. She had the means to acquire acknowledged masterpieces if that had been her ambition, yet Duke was not

**opposite**

*The Iranian dealer A. Rabenou not only sold historic works of art to Doris Duke, he also oversaw the creation of tile panels custom-made for Shangri La. He sent photographs of the work in progress, and penned notes on the reverse sides. On this photograph he wrote that he was overseeing the tile work as it was proceeding on March 20, 1939, in Isfahan.*

**above**

Tile panel (detail).

ISFAHAN, IRAN, 1938–1940. Glazed stone-paste, Courtyard, 48.93.

*David Franzen*

compelled to collect what others deemed worthy. Instead, her primary concern seems to have been to create Shangri La as a home first and foremost, a haven within which she could comfortably retreat from the pressures of celebrity. In some deeply personal way, the beauty of Islamic art filled her need for peace and solace. Duke collected works of art for the pleasure they gave her, not for their potential social prestige or monetary value.

Duke did acquire a number of masterpieces along her aesthetic journey. Taken as a whole, however, the Islamic art collection at Shangri La calls for a multifaceted interpretation, one that includes but is not limited to the assessment of apparent masterpieces. For example, the collection advocates study of the relatively unknown period of art production and patronage in the early twentieth century. Also, because Duke took an "assemblage" approach in displaying diverse works of Islamic art and architecture, Shangri La exemplifies the assemblage of cultures that are often included in the monolithic term "Islamic art." Since Duke followed her own ideas of what to collect, and not just what others or the art market deemed worthy, her collection is unlike any other available for study. It includes Islamic court arts, yet it also includes less familiar objects, such as those made for noble and consumer classes. The quality of these works invites discussion and evaluation of what constitutes "Islamic art." Although Shangri La could be studied as an Orientalist monument, Duke's decision to collect objects made in Europe for Muslim consumers suggests that the collection might just as fruitfully be studied for insights into "Occidentalism." Shangri La offers scholars and connoisseurs of Islamic art and art history an opportunity to look with fresh eyes at what is studied and how it is interpreted. Taking a wide-ranging approach to understanding the collection is rather like Duke's own inclusive approach to building it.

# Deciphering the Layers of Shangri La ———

As a place for the study of Islamic art and culture, as mandated in Doris Duke's will, Shangri La presents a complex set of challenges, including intellectual, interpretive, and aesthetic ones. What can be said of a young American woman, herself not a Muslim but a keen admirer of Islamic cultures, and her dream to collect Islamic art in the 1930s? What can be said of her designing and building a house in Hawaiʻi, using architectural principles and art forms from throughout the Islamic world? Further, what is meant by the monolithic term "Islamic world"—a simple phrase that can obscure a diversity of cultures, traditions, and aesthetics—and how does Shangri La help us to understand such diversity? In a way, Duke herself addressed this last question by variously calling her home "Near Eastern," "Hispano-Moresque," and even a "Spanish-Moorish-Persian-Indian complex." She most likely recognized that all these identities are part of Shangri La—as they are of the Islamic world itself.

Visitors to Shangri La may find that the site prompts more questions than it provides answers. It offers several layers of possible inquiry. In addition to Islamic architectural traditions, other styles are discernible. The estate demonstrates principles of modern architecture, a movement gaining currency at the time Shangri La was built. Various levels of floor changes and the integration of the house into the environment are reminiscent of Frank Lloyd Wright's homes; the descending glass wall recalls Mies van der Rohe's Tugendhat House; the overall asymmetric plan and the low, geometric structures are all characteristic of the modernist ethos. Yet the house also demonstrates aspects of Spanish/Mediterranean Revival styles in the overall sprawl of the buildings and gardens, the white walls, and the use of roof tiles and balconies.[37]

Part of Shangri La's cultural identity is most certainly Hawaiian. Its physical location, its landscaping, and its ocean and Diamond Head views continually remind visitors that this is no place but Hawaiʻi. Although there is currently little on display that reminds one of the material culture of Hawaiʻi, at one time Duke incorporated Shangri La's locale into her design of the dining room. Surfboards, painted barware, shell necklaces, and other locally produced objects can be found at Shangri La, but they are stored in the basement, in cupboards, and in drawers. Duke used these functional objects in her daily life, rather than using them as decoration in the house.

*The view from the dining room lānai.*

David Franzen

Shangri La can also be seen as a product of American upper-class culture whose extremely wealthy citizens, particularly at the turn of the twentieth century, built sensational seasonal homes for themselves. Typically these homes were located in socially sanctioned resort towns, such as Newport, Rhode Island, and Palm Beach, Florida. Shangri La was a seasonal home for Duke, and in some ways it reflects the idea of re-creating foreign architecture on American land. Well-known examples of this trend can be seen in Newport (the Vanderbilts' Italian-style villa, The Breakers, and their French-style mansion, Marble House), and in Palm Beach, where the Stotesburys built the Spanish-style El Mirasol. Duke's preference for the relatively remote location of Honolulu and a breadth of Islamic architectural traditions, not just Spanish, suggests that she partly accepted and partly rejected the formula established by her peers.

Shangri La can also be interpreted from the perspective of

American Orientalism. Duke was born in an era when ideas of the "Orient" were increasingly available to American consumers through movies, international expositions, advertising, imported goods, and even architectural design. To what extent was Duke affected by these visual representations of the "Orient"? How do her travels compare to the experiences of American artists, such as Frederic Church and Louis Comfort Tiffany, whose visits to the East in the nineteenth century also gave rise to a lifetime of creative responses?[38] Shangri La can shed considerable light on the phenomenon of visual culture and American Orientalism from the 1930s forward, which has so far received little critical attention.[39]

Finally, and perhaps most important, Shangri La must be seen as a product of Doris Duke herself. Although analyzing objects and formulating theories may contribute to an understanding of Shangri La, in the end its creator must be carefully considered in any interpretation. She decided to build, she determined which objects would be purchased, and she decided how they should be displayed. Architects and artisans contributed to Shangri La's appearance, but Duke was the only constant contributor throughout its sixty-year development. What did she seek to accomplish at Shangri La? Why did she decide to build a home of Islamic art in Hawai'i? Such questions may never be fully answered, for Duke left little in the way of personal writings to provide clues. However, Shangri La itself provides visual clues about Duke's motivation, and her staff and friends provide insights as well. For example, in walking around Shangri La and listening to her staff share memories,

*Among the locally produced objects Duke acquired is this barware set made c. 1940. Each hand-painted glass shows a different Hawaiian scene, such as surfing, canoeing, and hula dancing.*

*Shuzo Uemoto*

one gains a strong impression of Duke's love for being engaged with life, for learning new skills, and for improving her mind and abilities. With both Islamic art and Hawaiʻi, Duke probably saw an opportunity to immerse herself in new cultures. Shangri La allowed her to test her creative skills and collaborate with professional artisans, architects, and others whom she admired.

As it was envisioned, built, and inhabited during Duke's life, Shangri La probably supported all of these interpretations, and our understanding of it need not be limited to just one. In fact, to do so is something of an injustice to the fluidity of its creation and evolution, and to the numerous hands that were involved in producing it. As Shangri La moves into a new phase and opens to the public and academic community, it will generate more identities and interpretations, including, as Duke herself wanted, an identity as a place for educating people about Islamic art and culture.

Doris Duke's last will and testament charges the Doris Duke Foundation for Islamic Art, which owns and manages Shangri La, with promoting and encouraging the study of Islamic art. Can a site imagined and created by a wealthy young American woman accomplish just that? Despite the fact that Duke was not Muslim herself, Shangri La does provide a thought-provoking introduction to Islamic cultures. For example, it demonstrates a variety of architectural contexts within which to understand Islamic art. While religious spaces are less well represented, numerous domestic ones are present. The Mughal-style garden, the Playhouse, and the tentlike dining room—although created on site by Duke—provide immediate visual tools for understanding garden, palace, and nomadic architectural forms found throughout the Islamic world. Examples of Islamic urban architecture are present through the estate's courtyard plan and the historic interiors that adjoin it. The collection boasts objects from Spain, Morocco, Egypt, Iran, Iraq, Turkey, India, Pakistan, Uzbekistan, and China, among other countries, from the earliest periods of the religion into the present. The presence of numerous beautifully made architectural forms from the twentieth century confirms that the superb artistic traditions of the past are vigorous and dynamic in the modern world. Doris Duke appreciated this fact, and participated in this tradition. Her legacy is Shangri La, a place that reveals the breadth and diversity of Islamic art.

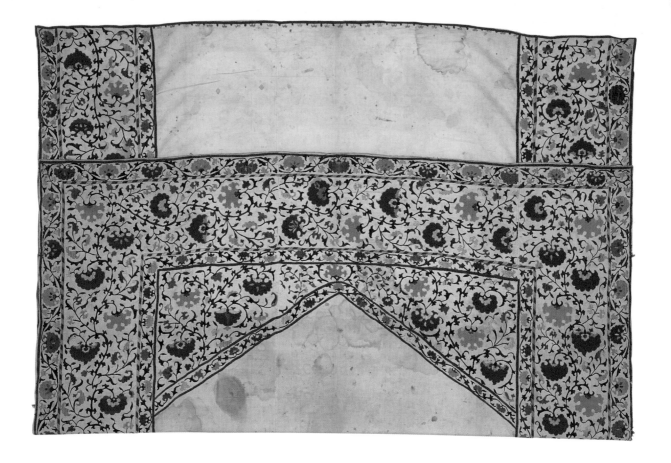

## Double-sided hanging (*suzani*).

CENTRAL ASIA, LATE NINE-
TEENTH CENTURY.
Linen, silk threads,
266.7 x 231.1 cm (105 x 91 in).
Storage, 85.55.

*Floral motifs abound in
Islamic art, and are often
associated with ideas
of paradise, well-being,
and other blessings. This
embroidery, heavily deco-
rated with multicolor floral
forms, is an example of
suzani, or "needlework."
Suzanis were made in
Central Asian towns and
villages, typically by a
mother for a daughter's
dowry. This bridal sheet
is a rare form, for it is
embroidered on both sides.*

*Shuzo Uemoto*

# Notes

1. Last Will and Testament of Doris Duke, Section Two, Part F, nos. 1–3.

2. Letter probably to Eva Stotesbury from James Cromwell, c. April 1935.

3. Letter to James Cromwell from F. B. Blomfield, July 4, 1935. Blomfield writes, "The floral design superimposed on the jali work will be different in each window. These floral designs are taken from the dado panels in the main entrance to the Taj."

4. Kazi Ashraf, review of Don J. Hibbard's manuscript on Shangri La, Honolulu, February 2002.

5. Letter to F. B. Blomfield from James Cromwell, May 22, 1935.

6. *Honolulu Advertiser*, September 19, 1935, 1, cols. 3–4.

7. Doris Duke, "My Honolulu House," *Town and Country*, August 1947, 73.

8. In the caption to the photograph of the undeveloped property at Ka'alāwai, the quotation from Anna Furtado Kahanamoku comes from a legal motion in the case of Doris Duke Cromwell vs. James Henry Roberts Cromwell, cited in Don J. Hibbard's "Shangri La: Doris Duke's Home in Hawaii," unpublished manuscript (November 2001), 246.

9. Letter to William D. Cross Jr. from James Cromwell, May 6, 1936.

10. See, for example, *Honolulu Star Bulletin*, August 6, 1936; December 3, 1936; February 20, 1937; and May 15, 1937; and *Honolulu Advertiser*, August 9, 1936; May 12, 1937; and June 27, 1937. For additional references, see Hibbard, "Shangri La."

11. *Honolulu Star Bulletin*, September 6, 1937, 1, cols. 4–6.

12. *Honolulu Star Bulletin*, September 24, 1938, 1, cols. 2–6.

13. "Life Goes Calling on Doris Duke Cromwell and Her Husband," *Life*, March 20, 1939, 74.

14. *Honolulu Star Bulletin*, September 24, 1938, 1, cols. 2–6.

15. The only comparable example was used in Mies van der Rohe's Tugendhat House of 1930 in Brno, Czechoslovakia.

16. Duke, "My Honolulu House," 75.

17. Guy T. Petherbridge, "Vernacular Architecture: The House and Society," in *Architecture of the Islamic World: Its History and Social Meaning*, ed. George Michell (London: Thames and Hudson, 1991), 176–210; Jennifer Scarce, *Domestic Culture in the Middle East: An Exploration of the Household Interior* (Edinburgh: National Museums of Scotland, 1996), 25–43.

18. Letter to William D. Cross Jr. from James Cromwell, May 6, 1936.

19. Scarce, *Domestic Culture in the Middle East*, 25–26; Petherbridge, "Vernacular Architecture," 200; Sheila S. Blair and Jonathan M. Bloom, *Images of Paradise in Islamic Art* (Hanover, N.H.: Hood Museum of Art, Dartmouth College, 1991), 106.

20. Letter to Doris Duke and James Cromwell from Mary Crane, June 14, 1938; letter probably to Doris Duke from Mary Crane, September 24, 1938.

21. Oral history interview with Johnny Gomez, conducted by William and Helen King, February 21, 1998.

22. Duke, "My Honolulu House," 77.

23. Kevorkian's gift to the Metropolitan Museum of Art is known as the Nur al-Din Room.

24. Oral history interviews with Jin de Silva, conducted by Sharon Littlefield, Ann Hayashi, and Laura Gorman, October 15 and 22, 1999.

25. Duke, "My Honolulu House," 73.

26. Cited in Hibbard, "Shangri La," 246.

27. In terms of size, Duke's collection is about the fifth largest in the United States. See Karin Adahl and Mikael Ahlund, *Islamic Art Collections: An International Survey* (Richmond, Surrey, England: Curzon Press, 2000).

28. Letters to Doris Duke and Marian Paschal from Mary Crane, June 22 and 30, 1940, and July 28, 1940.

29. Duke, "My Honolulu House," 75.

30. Receipt for James Cromwell from C. J. Baban, Charsoo St., Julfa, Isfahan, Iran, April 13, 1938.

31. See, for example, Mikhail B. Piotrovsky and John Vrieze, eds., *Earthly Art and Heavenly Beauty: Art of Islam* (Amsterdam: Lund Humphries Publishers, 2000), 155.

32. Western Union cablegram to A. Rabenou from Arthur Upham Pope, January 24, 1938.

33. A similar reproduction was displayed at a 1931 exhibition of Persian art in London. See B. W. Robinson, "The Burlington House Exhibition of 1931: A Milestone in Islamic Art History," in *Discovering Islamic Art: Scholars, Collectors, and Collections, 1850–1950*, ed. Stephen Vernoit (London: I. B. Tauris Publishers, 2000), 148.

34. Translation of a letter to William Dodsworth from A. Rabenou, June 18, 1939.

35. Hibbard, "Shangri La," 23–24.

36. See, for example, Victoria Kastner, *Hearst Castle: The Biography of a Country House* (New York: Harry N. Abrams, 2000), 52–53. A panel at the 2002 national conference of the College Art Association explicitly addressed the American aristocracy's collecting preferences: "The 'Golden Age' of American Art Collecting: Self-Serving Public Relations, Legacy Building, or Public Philanthropy," organized by Eric Zafran and Aaron De Groft.

37. Ashraf, review of Hibbard, 3–4.

38. Holly Edwards, ed., *Noble Dreams, Wicked Pleasures: Orientalism in America 1870–1930* (Princeton, N.J., and Williamstown, Mass.: Princeton University Press and Sterling and Francine Clark Art Institute, 2000), 31.

39. Ibid. Also, John Sweetman, *The Oriental Obsession: Islamic Inspiration in British and American Art and Architecture 1500–1920*, Cambridge Studies in the History of Art (Cambridge: Cambridge University Press, 1991).